The Ef
A Skills Development Series

Developing a
Parish Program

BY RICHARD REICHERT

RICHARD REICHERT
SERIES EDITOR

NATIONAL CONFERENCE OF
CATECHETICAL LEADERSHIP

Loyola Press

**NATIONAL CONFERENCE OF
CATECHETICAL LEADERSHIP**

3021 Fourth Street, N.E.
Washington, D.C. 20017-1102
1-202-636-3826

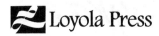Loyola Press

3441 North Ashland Avenue
Chicago, Illinois 60657
1-800-621-1008

Acknowledgments:
Cover Design: Shar Coulson Design

ISBN: 0-8294-1059-7

03 VGR   5 4 3 2

Table of Contents

About This Series   iv

Introduction   vi

**Chapter 1: Developing a Catechetical
          Program—An Overview**   1

**Chapter 2: Components of a Comprehensive
          Program**   12

Chapter 3: Putting the Pieces Together   26

**Chapter 4: Developmental Stages and
          Catechetical Structures**   37

Chapter 5: Programming for Adults   45

Conclusion   56

For Further Reading   57

About This Series

The Effective DRE: A Skills Development Series has been developed by the National Conference of Catechetical Leadership (NCCL) to help DREs and those preparing to become DREs to acquire the basic competencies required to be effective in the ministry. We recognize that the term DRE will mean different things in different dioceses throughout the country. We use the term DRE here as broadly as possible and intend it to refer to anyone involved in or planning to become involved in a leadership capacity in a parish religious education program. The actual scope of the leadership position can range from responsibility for the total program to responsibility for a particular portion of it, such as the task of serving as the coordinator for a junior high or senior high program. Thus the booklets, though addressed specifically to DREs, are designed to be of assistance to all parish catechetical leaders regardless of the title assigned to them or the scope of their job description.

The material in the booklets is based on the *National Certification Standards for Professional Parish Directors of Religious Education,* a document developed by the NCCL and approved by the United States Catholic Conference Commission on Certification and Accreditation. The *Standards* document is quite extensive and identifies and explains a wide range of skill and knowledge areas. We did not attempt to cover all of them in these booklets. Instead we used two criteria in deciding what topics to develop.

First, we sought to identify some of the most essential skill/knowledge areas, namely those most needed by anyone in a catechetical leadership position (such as recruiting and training volunteers or developing a program). Second, we sought to identify topics where information is not as readily available. For example, topics like knowledge of Scripture, theology, or expertise in the areas of catechetical methodology and conscience formation, though clearly essential to any catechetical leader, are topics about which much has already been written. So we chose instead to offer help with other important but less frequently discussed topics (such as budgeting and keeping records or maintaining personal balance).

Authored by experienced DREs and religious education professionals, the booklets provide practical advice, proven methods, and specific procedures for carrying out the many essential tasks related to directing a parish religious education program.

The series can be used as a resource in a formal diocesan ministry training program or in a small group study program. It can also be used by an individual for self-study. The entire series provides a comprehensive study program. Or, since each booklet is self-contained, persons may study only those booklets dealing with the skills they wish to improve.

Finally, the booklets can be kept on the DRE's resource shelf to be referred to whenever help is needed in carrying out a particular task.

Introduction

Program development requires calling on virtually all the knowledge and skills a DRE is asked to acquire: the nature, purpose, and content of catechesis as outlined in various Church documents; theory of the stages of faith and psychological development; familiarity with methodology; sociological principles regarding family life and the family life cycle; and sensitivity to a multicultural population and to those with special needs.

In this booklet we will review the principles and process for pulling all these together to complete the task of developing a comprehensive catechetical program for a parish. In chapter one we will look at the importance of developing a mission statement for your program. In chapter two we will review all the various qualities and components you need to consider in putting together a program as well as the implications of each. In chapter three we'll help you "put it all together" by outlining a process for actually developing a program. In chapter four we will examine some special concerns that need to be addressed when developing programs for children and youth. Finally, in chapter five we will review some special considerations regarding the development of catechetical programs for adults.

It is our hope that this material will provide both the theory and the practical suggestions you need either in developing a program from scratch or in evaluating and refining an already existing program.

1 Developing a Catechetical Program— An Overview

Perhaps the most fundamental responsibility of a DRE is to develop the parish's overall catechetical program. The *National Certification Standards* describes this responsibility by stating that the DRE must be able to "articulate a vision of comprehensive catechesis" and "design appropriate programs and curriculum for adults, adolescents, and children" (*Standards*, #535.01, 535.02).

The first step in doing this task successfully is to have a clear understanding of what is meant by the word program. Most simply, a catechetical program is a means to an end. In that sense it is much like a machine one constructs to produce a particular product. The nature of the machine you build is determined by the kind of end product you hope to produce.

THE IMPORTANCE OF THE MISSION STATEMENT

You begin to develop a catechetical program, therefore, by first formulating a clear picture (a vision or mission statement) of what it is you hope to achieve. Drawing on your own study of the nature and purpose of catechesis as found in the various Church documents [e.g., the *General Directory for Catechesis* (the revised version of the *General Catechetical Directory*), *Sharing the Light of Faith:*

*National Catechetical Directory for Catholics of the United
States, To Teach As Jesus Did, On Catechesis in Our Time,* and
so forth] you need to articulate a simple and clear statement of what you are seeking to accomplish. Here is a
sample of such a statement:

> The catechetical program of St. Matthew Parish
> seeks to provide adults, youth, and children with
> the knowledge, experiences, and skills necessary
> to become faithful and fruitful disciples of Jesus.
> In keeping with their age, they will assume
> responsibility as vital members of the parish and
> be able to participate in the Church's mission to
> proclaim, celebrate, and serve the coming of
> God's reign.

Do not underestimate the power of a mission statement
to shape your catechetical program. In the above sample,
much will depend on how you understand its key words
like "disciple." For example, Fr. Don Senior describes a
disciple as one who walks with, learns from, and participates
in the mission of Jesus, within a community of disciples.
Using that understanding you will shape your programming questions accordingly. For example, how does one
walk with Jesus today? Through prayer, pondering the
Scriptures, participating in the sacraments, associating
with other disciples? What are the vision and values of
Jesus a disciple seeks to learn? Answering that question is
what will shape much of the content or curriculum of your
program. What is the mission of Jesus and how does one
participate in it today? Who makes up the community of
disciples and what is involved in being a member of such
a community? Likewise, each of the words in "proclaim,
celebrate, and serve the coming of God's reign" is fraught
with meaning that needs to be explored as you shape
your program.

ASKING THE RIGHT QUESTIONS

Guided by a good mission statement, you can begin to ask the right program development questions. For example, what kinds of knowledge, experiences, and skills are needed by a particular age group to help them become the kind of disciples described? In what ways can this be done? Formal classes? Field trips? Small group experiences? Prayer experiences? Family activities? Liturgical celebrations? Intergenerational activities? Service projects? How much time is needed to achieve a specific goal? What facilities, instructional materials, or other resources are needed? What are the appropriate methodologies? What kind of training will the catechists need? What role will parents be expected to play? Answering these kinds of questions forms the foundation for developing a program.

So program development begins with a clear, comprehensive mission statement that embodies your vision and understanding of catechesis. Such a mission statement must be rooted in the documents that summarize the Church's catechetical tradition. You should also be careful to clearly situate the ministry of catechesis within the larger mission of the parish and the Church, because catechesis itself is a means to that greater end.

Often when a DRE is called to serve in a parish, it already has a catechetical mission statement. If that is your situation, review the existing mission statement carefully. Does it meet the criteria (comprehensive, rooted in tradition, related to the Church's overall mission) suggested above? Since your catechetical program is a means to an end, does the existing mission statement express the end you think needs to be achieved? Does it give you sufficient focus to begin to ask your programming questions? Is its language still timely, easily understood by the average parish member? In short, does it still serve as an adequate foundation for developing a catechetical program or does it need to be revised?

In any event, never launch into program development until you have a clear understanding of what you—and the parish leadership—expect the program to accomplish. If you are new to the parish, it is quite appropriate for you to seek clarification regarding the existing catechetical mission statement and to tactfully suggest amendments or revisions you feel might be necessary.

Here is one more caution. Before you begin developing a program be careful to remember that it will not exist in a vacuum. Remember that any program you develop needs to function as a partner to the many other parish ministries and activities that are also fostering growth in discipleship. Therefore, as much as possible, seek the advice and collaboration of the other parish ministries when developing your mission statement and establishing your goals. Your program should seek to utilize rather than compete with existing formative and instructional experiences already available, such as the Sunday liturgy, the justice and peace projects promoted by the social concerns committee, and youth ministry events if the youth ministry program is distinct from your catechetical program. The old adage "there's no need to reinvent the wheel" is a good principle to respect as you enter into program development.

DEVELOPING A PROGRAM: SEVERAL SCENARIOS

Assuming you inherit or are able to develop an adequate mission statement, there are several possible scenarios in which you might find yourself in terms of actual program development. First, you may be entering a parish that already has an existing program. In that case the remainder of the chapters in this booklet can be used to help you evaluate it. After evaluating the program, you may find you are one of the fortunate DREs who have inherited a highly developed and effectively functioning program. In such a happy circumstance, your program development task will be to facilitate the continued growth of the existing program by drawing on your leadership and administrative skills and the other necessary competencies you have developed related to the ministry.

On the other hand, as is often the case, you will inherit a program that is basically sound, but may need updating or adjusting to bring it in line with some changing circumstance of the parish or recent developments in catechesis. Being able to recognize the need for and then make such adjustments in an existing program is an integral skill of program development that you will be called on to employ often. Perhaps there has been a significant increase or decrease in the parish population or a shift in its ethnic or socioeconomic makeup since the existing program was first developed. Or the textbooks may have become outdated. Or there has been a change in budget and/or the availability of facilities. Maybe the diocese has introduced a new policy regarding the age of confirmation or the parish now needs a children's catechumenate.

Sometimes the programming adjustment may seem minor, like the need to update textbooks or the need to change the time groups meet to adjust to changes in the availability of facilities. Experience warns, however, that even the slightest changes can be very upsetting to those affected. Your veteran catechists, for example, may have become quite comfortable with the old textbooks and may resist the attempt to introduce a new or revised series. Parents often object to schedule changes, no matter how minor they may seem to you, because they conflict with existing family patterns.

Therefore, when faced with the need to introduce certain changes in an existing program, call on all the

knowledge and skills you have been able to acquire
regarding the correct processes for introducing change.
These include:

- moving slowly
- consulting sensitively and attentively with those
  who are most affected by the proposed changes
- communicating in every possible way the
  reasons for the proposed changes
- checking often to be certain the reasons are
  accurately understood
- going through proper channels to ensure the
  support of the parish leadership

If you are patient, sensitive, and reasonable, you can
usually take any good existing program and develop it into
a better one.

   Finally, there are times when you are either asked by
the parish leadership to develop a new program or when
you yourself see the need to abandon an existing program
and initiate a new one. In such a situation the remainder
of this booklet should prove very useful. In addition to the
principles and guidelines we will be offering, however, be
sure to look to another invaluable resource, namely the
other parishes in your diocese. With the help of your
DRE network and the diocesan staff, seek to identify
parishes of similar size and demographic makeup that are
known to have successful catechetical programs. Arrange
to visit these parishes and consult with their DREs. Many
times you will find well-developed programs or portions
of a program you can adopt with little or no adaptation.
Do not be embarrassed to seek such help, especially if you
are just starting out in the ministry. Also, do not hesitate
to seek the advice of your diocesan religious education
office staff, both in the development of your program and
in critiquing your plans before you begin implementation.

Their familiarity with diocesan policy and their overall expertise in the field of catechesis are invaluable aids in your work.

When it is necessary to develop a new program for a parish, also be sure to assemble a consultative group. This can be considered essential if you are new to the parish. It should be made up of some veteran catechists, a representative group of parents and appropriate members of the parish staff, especially any who are directing the ministries with which you will need to work closely, such as liturgy, social concerns, or youth ministry. For certain aspects of the program, such as the segment designed for the youth of the parish, you will want to seek input from them. While it is true that you bear the major responsibility for program development, this consultative group plays an essential role. Ask them to react to your ideas as you formulate them, seek their advice in resolving problems and conflicts, and employ them as a sounding board to test how the parish at large will react to your proposals.

Besides its obvious benefit of providing you with valuable information and feedback, this consultative group becomes your ally when it is time to seek the acceptance and support of the total parish. Those who have been made to feel a part in the planning process will assume ownership of the program once it is developed and will help to promote its adoption.

A WORD ABOUT ALTERNATIVE MODELS

When it comes to program development there is much talk today in catechetical circles about developing alternative models. Unfortunately there is also a great deal of confusion about what is meant by an "alternative model." Shifting schedules, extending or shortening class time, and adding creative experiences to the routine, no matter how creative these changes may be, are basically innovations in the existing program. This is not the same as truly creating an alternative way to carry out catechetical ministry.

To develop an authentic alternative model implies that you must first radically rethink the mission of catechesis and/or the presuppositions related to carrying it out. For example, much of catechetical programming today is driven by a vision or mission statement related to providing religious instruction. In the same way much of the methodology used is designed to *inform* more than it is designed to *form*. These are time honored approaches and have much in their favor. But as long as you begin with these kinds of presuppositions, whatever program you develop will at best be made up of innovations on existing programs that start from the same premises.

To develop truly alternative programs, therefore, you need to begin with a different set of presuppositions. For example, by using discipleship rather than religious instruction as your goal, you immediately shift focus from imparting information about Jesus and the Church to forming a relationship with Jesus and with the community of disciples. The methods you would use to foster relationships will be quite different than those you would use to impart information. Likewise, overall structures would shift from a classroom model to a more intimate small group format. Catechists would be trained more as facilitators of reflection and less as teachers. Intergenerational groupings would be added to traditional groupings by chronological age or "class." You would approach the task of selecting resources and instructional materials, such as textbooks, much differently.

By stating this we are not advocating that traditional forms of catechetical programming be abandoned and be replaced by the type just described. We simply want to stress that there is an important distinction between introducing innovations, no matter how creative, into an existing program model and developing a truly alternative program. Such a truly alternative program requires the kind of radical shift in vision and fundamental principles mentioned above. Introducing such a truly alternative program is much more challenging, therefore, than introducing innovations in an existing one.

To get an idea of what a truly alternative model implies, consider Vatican II. In a real sense it was an attempt to introduce a new way of being Church, calling us to shift from the more traditional hierarchical model to a communal model using the biblical image of the People of God. It also called us to be less concerned with survival, more open to cooperation with people of other Christian and non-Christian faiths, and more committed to the evangelical mission of proclaiming the Good News of God's reign, especially through witnessing and doing works on behalf of justice and peace. The implications of these seemingly minor changes in ecclesiology are enormous, and almost 30 years later you can still find significant resistance to embracing them.

In introducing a truly alternative model, then, you must first educate parish leadership, parents, and catechists to think of the Church and catechesis in a whole new way. Such education can be akin to asking for conversion, a letting go of familiar, comfortable, and seemingly effective ways of thinking and acting, much like the kind of conversion Vatican II called us to embrace. And resistance to such a conversion can be every bit as deeply rooted.

We don't want to discourage you if you experience the need to develop a truly alternative program in your parish. Just be forewarned that it is a major task. It not only requires tact and patience but demands that you carefully prepare a theological and catechetical rationale that will justify developing a truly alternative model and that you determine ways to communicate these effectively to the parish community.

SUMMARY

A catechetical program is a means to an end and will be shaped by the end it is designed to achieve, much like a machine is designed in keeping with the product it is to make. So the foundation of program development is one's catechetical mission statement. The more time you spend reflecting on and then articulating your catechetical mission, the easier the task of program development becomes.

The mission statement guides you in asking the right programming questions: What activities must we use to achieve this goal? How much time will be needed? What kinds of resources will be needed? How should people be grouped? What kind of training is required? What role do parents need to play in achieving this goal? How do these activities relate to the core mission? Answering these questions is key to program development.

The task of program development can range from simply maintaining a good program you inherited, to making adjustments in an existing program, to starting from scratch. In any of these instances, the principles, guidelines, and suggestions found in the remainder of this booklet can aid you well.

Finally, keep in mind the important distinction between developing creative innovations in an existing program model and developing a truly alternative program model. The latter requires a radical shift in how you view catechesis and will be much more challenging than simply introducing innovations into an existing program. Therefore, if you do choose the route of developing a truly alternative model, proceed with patience and take care to "do your homework" first.

FOR REFLECTION:

1. How well do you think your parish's present catechetical mission statement serves as a guide for program

development? What might be added or better stated in it? What are the "programming questions" it suggests? Are these adequate?

2. If your parish presently does not have a catechetical mission statement, gather some interested people and attempt to develop one in keeping with the principles outlined above.

3. How would you describe the difference between developing an authentic alternative model and altering an existing program?

2 Components of a Comprehensive Program

Not only is program development the most fundamental responsibility of the DRE, it also is the most
comprehensive, calling on you to use virtually all the
training and skills you are expected to acquire in your
preparation for the ministry. This will become more obvious to you as we review the various areas of concern you
need to consider in the process of program development.
You will find these qualities and components for a good
program listed in the *National Certification Standards*,
#535.01–535.ll. Before we review them, however, we need
to make a few clarifications.

First, because parishes come in all shapes and sizes, each
with a unique set of assets and limitations, each parish's
catechetical program has a certain unique quality. If that
were not the case there would be no need to be concerned
about program development. One program could be used
in all parishes, in a kind of "one size fits all" approach. As
it is, each program has to be tailored to meet the needs of
the parish for which it is designed. So as we review the
various elements found in a comprehensive program, keep
in mind that they will not all be of equal importance to
you in tailoring a program for your own parish.

For example, a good program will be sensitive to multicultural needs. This will be a major consideration in any
parish made up of many diverse racial and ethnic groups,
such as is common in some of our larger cities and in areas
like the West and East Coasts, which have large immigrant

populations. While multicultural sensitivity is still required in a program designed for a small rural parish with a homogeneous population, it does not pose the same challenges as in the kinds of parishes just mentioned.

Second, a review of these qualities and components can be used in two ways. On the one hand, if you have inherited an existing program you can evaluate it in light of the following list of criteria to see if anything essential is missing or is underdeveloped. On the other hand, if you are charged with developing a program from scratch, this chapter can serve as an important guide to ensure you are in fact developing a comprehensive program.

1. THE PROGRAM HAS A WELL-ARTICULATED VISION

In the first chapter we have already treated at length the first component. Namely, a good program will be driven by a well-articulated mission statement that is rooted in a thorough understanding of the nature and purpose of catechesis and its relation to the overall mission of the Church, as these have been explained in the major catechetical documents (#535.01). Here we simply want to underscore the importance of this component. No matter what the makeup of the parish you serve, a well-developed mission statement needs to be the foundation of the program.

This presumes you have acquired a solid understanding of the nature of catechesis and can articulate it effectively. Equipped with that understanding you will find that the other programming tasks become more or less instinctive. If your thinking remains fuzzy in this regard, the rest of your programming is likely to suffer. The implication here is that to be effective in your ministry you will need to continually strive to deepen and refine your understanding of catechesis by reading the professional literature in the field and by attending workshops and formal classes whenever possible.

2. THE PROGRAM HAS A WELL-DESIGNED CURRICULUM

The key to approaching this component is a proper understanding of what is meant by curriculum. Presuming your mission statement identifies a catechetical goal that goes beyond imparting information to include the development of conscience, values, and a Gospel-driven lifestyle, your curriculum needs to be more than a scope and sequence that lists the information to be taught and when it will be taught. It also needs to identify the values and behaviors to be acquired.

A good curriculum, therefore, is at the heart of program development. It seeks to translate the overarching goal of catechesis into sets of specific, measurable goals to be achieved at a particular age or by a particular group of people. There is a curriculum or set of goals for children preparing for first Eucharist, for example, and another for youth preparing for confirmation. There is a curriculum or set of goals appropriate for adults, another for junior high youth, and so forth.

As is true with so much of program development, there is no need to reinvent the wheel. There is a good chance your diocesan office has established a curriculum to assist you. The various major textbook series provide well-researched scope and sequence charts that are useful starting points when developing a curriculum for children and youth. The *General Directory for Catechesis* and *Sharing the Light of Faith: National Catechetical Directory for Catholics of the United States* provide similar lists of goals to guide you. You can also consult with parishes in your area that have well-established programs to see how they have organized their curriculum.

The recently published *Catechism of the Catholic Church* is, of course, to be considered an essential resource in developing and evaluating both the overall curriculum and the content of specific topics to be presented. As a point of information, there is now an Office for the Catechism, established by the U.S. bishops, that has developed a "Protocol for Assessing the Conformity of Catechetical Materials with the *Catechism of the Catholic Church.*" The office is reviewing existing and forthcoming catechetical textbook series in light of this protocol. The results of these reviews can be very helpful in your efforts to identify an appropriate program.

Ultimately, you need to adapt any of these resources to meet the needs and circumstances in your parish. For example, many small parishes find it necessary to group several classes together, such as seventh and eighth grade youth. This calls for a curriculum designed slightly differently than if these youth gathered separately. If you opt for a youth ministry model with all high school youth together, your curriculum cannot mirror one designed for catechizing youth in formal classes grouped by age. The age at which your parish/diocese prepares youth for confirmation will also affect your curriculum design.

In any event, there are several principles to guide you in developing your curriculum:

- First, do not be overly ambitious. It is much better to identify three or four goals you can achieve with a particular age group than to list ten or twelve goals that, no matter how admirable, have the effect of discouraging you and your catechists and setting you up for apparent failure.

- Second, before you list any goal, you should have at least a general idea of how you hope to achieve it. In other words, your goals should match your resources. For example, it does no good to list as a goal providing a youth retreat unless you can realistically develop a plan for doing so.
- Third, make sure your goals are developmentally appropriate. This latter principle is actually one of the basic elements in program development identified by the *Standards* (#535.03 and 535.041), and we will address it next.

3. THE PROGRAM IS DEVELOPMENTALLY APPROPRIATE AND USES APPROPRIATE METHODS

As noted, here we are combining two of the criteria listed in the *Standards*. All the developmental theory, catechetical methodology, and learning styles theory that you study as you prepare to be a DRE have their practical application in this aspect of program development. Stated simply, your program's structure and, in particular, its curriculum need to match the capacities, learning styles, and readiness of the age group being catechized. This applies both to content and to methods. For example, the use of independent study as a method is more appropriate for high school youth and adults than for children in the primary grades. Careful attention to various learning styles ensures that visual, auditory, and kinesthetic learners' needs are met with approaches appropriate to their skill and ability levels.

Many errors in applying developmental theory occur in the area of curriculum. Often, complex and abstract concepts are introduced too soon when the children or youth still lack the capacity to grasp them. Just as often, the program calls for using methods that don't match the developmental stage. Lecturing, debate, small group discussion, and "research projects" can all have a place when used with older youth and adults. They are for the most part useless with smaller children in the primary grades.

Your knowledge of developmental theory is especially important when selecting textbooks and other resources. In general all mainstream textbook series employ current developmental theory in their design, but some series tend to err by being too ambitious, introducing certain concepts too early in their scope and sequence. Others err by not being challenging enough. Since the perfect series is yet to be written, this means that if you adopt a textbook series, you will usually still have to do some adapting by either deleting or adding to the goals and content provided.

Finally, this principle has special significance in programming for adults. Adults' needs and their learning style differ greatly from children and younger youth. We will be saying more about this in a later chapter when we deal specifically with programming for adult catechesis.

4. THE PROGRAM IS BASED ON NEEDS ASSESSMENT AND IMPLEMENTS ONGOING EVALUATION

Once again we are combining two of the elements listed in the *Standards* (#535.041 and 535.05). Needs assessment should take place before program planning. Evaluation takes place once the program is operating. Both are important. Needs assessment is periodic; evaluation should be ongoing. Needs assessment seeks to discern various aspects of the parish and its members. It involves tangible elements such as demographics and socioeconomic make-up. How many elderly are in the parish, how many young adults, how many persons with special needs, physical or developmental disabilities, how many single-parent families or blended families? What is the average education level of the adults? What is the ethnic and racial composition of the parish?

Needs assessment also involves discernment of less tangible but observable aspects of the parish. Does racial tension exist? Does the parish neighborhood have a drug problem, a youth gang problem, a high unemployment rate? Is it considered a safe place to live? Is the parish ensconced in a comfortable suburb and turned in on itself? What is its present commitment to evangelization, to service, to pursuing works of justice and peace?

Needs assessment addresses the parish's internal life. What is the present quality of the liturgy? How do the parishioners relate to their pastor and the parish staff? Are there noticeable tensions or factions in the parish? What facilities are available, and what is their condition? If the parish operates a school, what is the relationship between it and the religious education program? How well do the parish council and the board of education understand the nature and role of catechesis in the parish. What ministries and organizations does the parish maintain, and what is their present relationship to the catechetical program?

Given the nature and scope of needs assessment as just described, much of this kind of information is readily available simply by attentive observation, interviews, reviewing parish records, and consulting with other members of the parish team. It does not require some sophisticated instrument or process. So how you gather this information is not as critical as how you use it.

In terms of program development some needs can be addressed by adding new components. For example, if you have a growing population of elders, you may want to initiate events that deal with their specific catechetical needs.

Other needs will suggest introducing a certain content into your program. For example, if your area is plagued with the problem of youth gangs or with a high incidence of teen pregnancy, you may need to give special attention to these issues when developing your youth program.

In using your needs assessment to help shape your program, there is an important principle to keep in mind. Stay within the parameters of your ministry. A catechetical program cannot address all the needs or solve all the problems a parish might experience. Some needs must be addressed by other ministries and organizations in the parish. If you have a concern with the quality of the parish's liturgy, for example, share your concern tactfully with the worship committee or other appropriate person or group. You can seek to foster greater understanding, appreciation, and participation in the liturgy through your program, but it is not your responsibility to "reform" the liturgical life of the parish and its celebrations.

Evaluation seeks to determine how well you have achieved the goals established through the process of curriculum development. The results of the evaluation will indicate if you need to change anything. For example, if attendance at adult programs is poor, you may have to look at your scheduling procedures, the formats you are using, the topics addressed, and how they were determined.

Unlike needs assessment, which is periodic, evaluation should, to a certain degree, be ongoing. If you discern early in the year that something is amiss, for example, a high degree of absenteeism in the youth program, you should not wait until the end of the year to address it. If through observation you realize a particular catechist is not suited for a particular age group, some immediate adjustment is called for. Early detection of problems is the primary benefit of ongoing evaluation. Though it is not always easy to make changes once a program is underway, the effort is worth it in terms of the overall success and smooth operation of the program you've established.

Here are some considerations for handling the evaluation aspect of your program. First, much ongoing evaluation can take place, as suggested, by simply remaining observant as the program unfolds during the year. Poor attendance, ongoing discipline problems, and specific complaints from parents or catechists are all clear warning signs that all is not well. When doing programs for adults, it is recommended that you always include a brief evaluation process at the end of the session or program. This enables you to make adjustments as you prepare for the next scheduled event.

Second, an "end of the year evaluation" needs to be more formal, but it can be handled in a variety of ways. It is not unreasonable to ask catechists to give tests related to the content presented (facts, concepts, definitions, and so forth). Assigning grades for this kind of cognitive achievement is not unreasonable either. Tests and grades can be a relatively reliable measure of how well cognitive goals have been achieved. You may want to check with your diocesan office when it comes to testing. Some dioceses have established certain "testing standards" that identify what a child is expected to have learned by a given grade level. In that way you can measure the effectiveness of your own program against diocesan norms and expectations. It is much more difficult, of course, to measure how well children, youth, and adults have acquired the values, attitudes, and habits of behavior you are seeking to foster.

Although evaluating responses remains a subjective process, you can solicit valuable information by conducting interviews, by asking older students to write testimonials, or by asking students to complete a questionnaire that deals with changes in attitudes and behavior. A simple form that requests students to identify the five most important things they learned or experienced in the year's program can itself be quite revealing.

Providing a similar form to parents is also effective. Ask them to evaluate the tangible elements of their child's program: convenience of schedule, the textbook used and the content presented, the appropriateness of the special experiences provided (retreat, field trip), and how well they were kept informed of events and of their child's progress. Include space for offering suggestions for changes. Also ask for a more subjective evaluation: What changes, if any, did they perceive in their child's attitude toward the faith, in his or her behavior? Did the child seem to enjoy or resent attending the program?

Seek similar feedback either through interviews or through a questionnaire from your catechists. How did they feel about the schedule, the content and instructional materials, the frequency and quality of the training experiences provided, the discipline policy, the quality and frequency of your communications with them, and the cooperation of parents? Would they want to teach again? Why or why not?

In the same way seek feedback from other members of the parish team. They are often in a position to see and hear things not available to you. What was their impression of the overall program? What do they consider its strong points and its weaknesses? How can it be better integrated into the overall life and activities of the parish? A simple questionnaire followed by a personal chat is the recommended procedure here.

Though time consuming, it is possible to get a great deal of feedback at the end of the year. The real challenge comes in processing the feedback because it will not all be of equal value. First, look for trends and patterns. Do not become distracted by highly vocal but isolated criticism. If the majority of parents and catechists seem satisfied, for example, do not overreact to the complaints of one or two persons, no matter how strongly presented. Isolated complaints usually indicate the problem lies more with the complainer than with the program. They are best dealt with on an individual basis, not by altering the entire program. Likewise, if the majority of children do well on an "end of the year test," you need not overreact to the disappointing performance of the few. If the whole group does poorly, of course, you will need to discern why and make appropriate adjustments.

Evaluation can be compared to getting physical check ups. You do not wait a year to see a doctor if you are suffering from a painful symptom right now. Likewise, even though you feel healthy it is wise to get an annual check up anyway, just in case. Use the same principles in evaluating the health of the program you develop.

5. THE PROGRAM RESPECTS THE DIVERSE NEEDS OF THE PARISH COMMUNITY

This component of program development flows from several articles cited in the *Standards* (#535.06, 535.07, and 535.08). If your parish has a multicultural makeup, the implications of this have to be incorporated into your planning. Likewise, you have to take into account the special needs of parish members who have physical or developmental disabilities. Finally, most parishes encompass a wide variety of family structures, each at a particular stage in the family life cycle.

As stated above in relation to needs assessment, do not feel it is your responsibility to answer every special need of every member of the parish. The key word here is respect, which implies a basic sensitivity you bring to your program development. Your program must be aimed at meeting the needs of the majority of the members in any particular group of children, youth, or adults. But as you go about designing your program you need to continually ask certain questions, such as: How can those with disabilities best be included in this aspect of the program? What special arrangements, if any, need to be made? How will this activity, method, or topic be perceived by the cultural minorities who will be participating? Will I need to give them some special instruction, explanation, or preparation so they will feel at ease and can benefit by it? Are my communications, meeting schedules, and parental involvement activities sensitive to the circumstances of single parents, parents in blended families, parents with large families still at home, and families where both parents work outside the home?

Again, you cannot hope to solve all problems and meet all the special needs present in the parish community. But you are expected to approach your program development with this kind of basic awareness and sensitivity to the diversity of the needs that do exist. As much as possible, you then seek to respect them, anticipate possible problems, and make whatever allowances you can without jeopardizing the effectiveness of the overall program.

6. THE PROGRAM INCORPORATES PRINCIPLES OF GOOD PUBLIC RELATIONS

Comprehensive DRE training will include instruction in the principles of public relations: effective written communication (brochures, letters, handbooks, etc.), effective oral communication (formal and impromptu speaking), and working with the media, all coordinated into a total plan of timely sharing of information.

Because much of this is covered elsewhere in this series (see the booklet entitled *Communicating Effectively*), we will not explore the topic here. We simply want to stress that a well-planned process and schedule for ongoing communication with parish leadership, parents, catechists, and the parish at large should be considered an integral part of your overall catechetical program. As Jesus taught, we should not light a candle and then keep it under a basket. Consider your public relations plan as the lampstand on which you place your program.

7. THE PROGRAM UTILIZES ALL AVAILABLE CURRENT TECHNOLOGY

This component of program development is addressed by the *Standards* in articles #535.10 and 535.11. Today's children and youth are often described as the media generation. In much the same way our whole society is now awash in a sea of electronic tools that it depends on heavily: the fax machine, computers, scanners, printers, copiers, e-mail, and the Internet. The majority of homes have several TVs, a VCR, a CD player, and a telephone answering machine.

Effective program development today, therefore, needs to take all this into account. For example, a good program will seek to incorporate the use of appropriate videos in its instructional material. Assuming you have access to a computer, printer, and copier (not always a valid assumption in many smaller parishes), these should be incorporated effectively into your communications process and your record keeping. Access to the Internet and e-mail is an invaluable tool in networking with others in the field and in seeking specific information. If nothing else, you will need some familiarity with the Internet simply to stay informed of the world in which your children and youth are growing up.

There is a subtle trap here, however. We can become so fascinated with our electronic equipment that it can distract us from, rather than assist us in, our tasks. For example, you could end up spending way too much time playing with a desktop publishing program attempting to design a really flashy brochure. So in seeking to incorporate the use of the latest technology in your program's development, keep asking this question: Am I using this equipment as a tool or a toy?

SUMMARY

Drawing on the *Standards* it is possible to identify a number of elements to be incorporated into your catechetical program. These can be used to evaluate an existing program, adjust a program, or develop one from scratch. While all are important, some may not have the same degree of relevance for your parish as others. Approach them accordingly. Finally, as noted, these elements touch on virtually all the skills and knowledge you are asked to acquire in your preparation to be a DRE. Thus, actual program development continues to become easier to the degree that you are able to continue to grow in all these other areas of responsibility.

For Reflection:

1. Given the circumstances and makeup of your parish, which of the program components do you feel need the greatest attention? Which ones do you feel are already rather well developed?

2. In developing or refining the program for your parish, do you think it is necessary to carry out a needs assessment first? Why or why not?

3. Given the description of the various qualities and components of an effective program, are there any areas in which you think you personally need more training? How do you propose to get that training?

3 Putting the Pieces Together

The place to start when actually developing a program—or reviewing an existing one—is to make a list of the distinct groups to be served. Though this list may vary from parish to parish, depending on the DRE's job description, the actual process will be the same. Typically it will include children in primary grades, middle school (or junior high), and high school. If you organize your program grade by grade, then list each grade level as a separate group. Your parish may also provide a preschool and kindergarten program.

Adult education may or may not be included, and this may include a young adult program. Often the RCIA and/or children's catechumenate program is the DRE's responsibility. Some parishes have a family life program. By dividing your total program into these smaller segments, you'll make the task of program development more manageable.

As you formulate your list, note the relevant information obtained from any needs assessment you carried out. For example, if teen pregnancy has become a problem in your area, you will want to remember to address that issue when developing a program for junior high and/or high school students. If there is a significant number of children with disabilities in the primary grades, you will want to remember to address that issue in your program.

STEP ONE: FORMULATE AN OVERALL GOAL, OBJECTIVES, AND OUTCOMES

For each group identified you need to formulate an overall goal and specific objectives that flow from it. These, of course, should be rooted in and flow from your mission statement. In the sample of the mission statement given in chapter one, discipleship was the emphasis. Here is a sample of an overall goal for sixth grade youth that flows from that mission statement and also identifies the main focus for that group, namely Scripture:

> **Grade level goal:** That the youth become familiar with the Hebrew Scriptures and their importance in the life of discipleship and in the life of the community of disciples, the Church.

You give this overall goal more precision by now identifying several more specific objectives. Here are the three objectives developed in relation to the above overall goal:

> **Objective one:** Disciples understand that the Hebrew Scriptures are foundational to the Christian tradition. Therefore, disciples are able to:

> **Objective two:** Disciples enter more fully into the liturgy of the Word at the celebration of the Eucharist, based on an increased awareness of the Scriptures. Therefore disciples are able to:

> **Objective three:** Disciples relate the message and moral values proclaimed by the Hebrew prophets with the message and moral values proclaimed by Jesus: justice, concern for the poor and helpless, fidelity to God's Law, and mercy and forgiveness. Therefore, disciples are able to:

You can see that good objectives break open the overall goal and also give direction to what will follow, namely specific outcomes you hope to achieve with this age group. Here is a sample of the list of outcomes that were developed in relation to objective two:

Outcomes: Disciples (the youth) are able to:

- recognize the various symbols from the Hebrew Scriptures that are now used by the Church in its liturgical celebrations: lamb, water, fire, oil, unleavened bread

- understand the relationship that exists between the Passover event in the Hebrew Scriptures and the Church's celebration of the Eucharist

- pray using the Hebrew Scriptures, especially the Psalms

This statement of outcomes is what ultimately determines the content and activities for this segment of your program. It is what drives the development of lesson plans, for example. There is, of course, a list of outcomes for each objective. Although formulating such a clear statement of goals, objectives, and learning outcomes is not easy, once the statement is completed it is valuable for several reasons:

1. It gives you clear direction in selecting appropriate resources and identifying suitable activities.

2. It gives clear direction to your catechists, telling them just what they are striving to achieve at any given point in the program. It also helps them better recognize the specific purpose of the learning activities/methods you suggest. Or if they develop their own lesson plans, it gives them the needed focus to do so effectively.

3. It is a useful statement to share with parents so they can see exactly what to expect from the year's program. In fact, it is highly recommended that you share such a list of goal, objectives, and outcomes with parents, including with it a list of practical ways they can (are expected to) help to achieve them.

4. It becomes the norm against which you evaluate the success of the program at the end of the year.

Here are a few guidelines to keep in mind. First, in developing your objectives and outcomes, always keep in mind the developmental level of the group on which you are focusing. Keep asking if it is realistic to expect this age group to achieve what you are listing. Second, do not be too ambitious. Three or four objectives are usually adequate. Also, do not get carried away in listing desired outcomes.

STEP TWO: IDENTIFY RELATED ACTIVITIES

Your next step is to list any special activities required for this group that will take place outside the regularly scheduled sessions or outside the normal facilities. For example, in designing the confirmation program such special activities might include the retreat experience, meetings with parents/sponsors, and a practice session for the ceremony itself. If you see the need to have any special parent sessions for a particular group, these should be listed. If you intend to hold a field trip or a parent/child session for a particular group, this should be listed.

Equipped with your statement of goal, objectives, and outcomes and this list of related activities, you are now ready for the next important step.

STEP THREE: DETERMINE YOUR PROCESS AND RESOURCES

Now that you know what you want to achieve in relation to a particular group, you can begin to ask the process and resource questions:

1. What catechist and student resources will I need to achieve the outcomes? Possible resources include a published textbook and catechist manual, videos and other audiovisuals, and guest presenters.

2. What should my overall structure be for this group? Formal classes, small group format (with or without facilitators)? A combination of large group, small group? Youth ministry model? Intergenerational model? Family-centered model?

3. How many sessions will I need for these gatherings? For related activities? What length should these sessions be?

4. Finally, what facilities will I need? Classroom, church hall, the church itself?

The answers to some of these questions should be determined by your own convictions and expertise. For example, if you are convinced that the small group model is preferred over the formal class model for this age group, that is how you should structure your program. The same will be true in selecting a textbook or other resources.

Some of these questions, however, are in a sense predetermined by the circumstances in your diocese or parish. Some dioceses, for example, require a minimum number of hours per year. Or if it is the tradition in the parish for groups to meet 25 times a year, between September and May, you may be confined to structure your program within that framework. Then the question becomes one of determining how many of those 25 sessions you assign to a particular objective or set of outcomes. You may, however, have some flexibility in determining how long some of these sessions are. Likewise, you may not have much choice in terms of facilities.

The answers to these questions give you a rather clear picture of some of the administrative tasks that lie ahead of you: ordering textbooks, scheduling facilities, arranging for guest speakers, and lining up the audiovisual material and equipment you will need. Knowing this kind of information well ahead of time will make the actual implementation of the program go much more smoothly.

STEP FIVE: PUTTING IT ALL TOGETHER

In developing a total program you would want to repeat the process outlined in steps 1–4 for each group or class. For example, you would develop a similar program for your confirmation preparation group, your first Communion group, and so forth. Assuming you intend to train catechists, it is a good idea to develop something similar for this segment of your program.

As you move from group to group, be careful to avoid unnecessary repetition in goals. Also, review the logic of the sequence you develop. If you are being guided by a textbook series this is not a concern. If you are developing your program from scratch or adapting an existing one, check the flow from group to group to ensure two things: first, that you are not missing some important area, and second, that there is a logical progression from the goal for one group and the goal for the next group.

Once you have developed a program for each of the groups for which you are responsible, you are ready for the final step: scheduling the total program. For the most

part, this task is self-explanatory, but here are a few guidelines to keep in mind:

1. Include in your overall schedule times for
   registration.
2. Include catechist training sessions and related
   meetings in your overall schedule.
3. Take into account major holidays and significant local events that affect youth or parents
   (e.g., a basketball tournament).
4. Combine activities as much as possible to
   minimize the need for parents to come out.
   For example, you can combine registration
   and a parent session in which you introduce
   them to the year's program and their
   responsibilities.
5. Coordinate your schedule with that of the
   school, if the parish has one, as well as all
   other regular parish activities. For example,
   you do not want to plan to use the church if
   the choir will be practicing in it at the same
   time.
6. Check on the availability of any facilities
   outside the parish you plan to use, such as a
   retreat center, before you schedule your
   event(s).

As you are probably aware, there is no ideal time for
scheduling sessions with children, youth, or their parents.
Much will depend on the circumstances in your area. For
example, an important consideration is whether younger
children can walk to the parish or must be driven there.
The number of students may be larger than the number of
rooms available at any one time, which certainly compli-
cates scheduling.

While Wednesday night is a rather traditional time to gather children and youth, some parishes have found that meeting less frequently but meeting for longer periods of time works for them, such as on a Sunday afternoon or evening. Some parishes conduct a summer school rather than holding sessions during the regular school year. Some have chosen to meet throughout the year, building the program around the liturgical seasons. Some parishes have younger children come on one day and older children on another. Of course, in scheduling you must always strive to be as "family friendly" as possible, being sensitive to possible conflicts today's busy parents might experience in adapting to your program's schedule. The point here is that you should not hesitate to be creative when you set about to establish a schedule.

Once you have succeeded in scheduling all the segments of your program and translating them into an official calendar for the year, your program development is almost complete. Two more tasks remain: developing an evaluation process and forming a public relations strategy.

STEP SIX: DETERMINE AN EVALUATION PROCESS

We described the possible processes for conducting an evaluation in an earlier chapter. Here we just want to remind you to include it in a formal way in your overall program. As mentioned, if you can develop a clear set of desired outcomes for each group in your program, these become a valuable and rather objective guide for conducting an evaluation.

How you choose to proceed—questionnaires, tests, interviews, and so forth—is up to you. Just remember to account for an evaluation in your program outline and to schedule a time for conducting it in your overall schedule. This not only ensures that it will be done, but it also alerts students, parents, and catechists that both you and they are going to be held accountable.

STEP SEVEN: DETERMINE A PROCESS TO INFORM ALL INVOLVED

The qualities of good public relations or PR in this area are these: it is comprehensive, providing all the information everyone involved needs, and it is timely, getting the information out well enough in advance for all participants to use it effectively. To ensure your PR planning meets these criteria you need to ask three questions:

1. Who needs to know about the program?
2. What parts of the program do they need to know about?
3. What ways should I use to inform them?

Students, parents, catechists, the parish team, the janitor, the school staff (if you have a school in the parish), and administrators of the local public schools where your children and youth attend—these are some of the people who need to know about your program. But not everyone needs to know the same thing. Parents and catechists involved in the first Communion program need to know the schedule of events and the goals designed for their children. The janitor only needs to know the schedule. The pastor and liturgist will need to know what will be expected of them in terms of practice and the celebration but may not have to know the rest of the particulars of the program. Finally, besides a general brochure that may provide an overview of the entire program and schedule, you need to anticipate what special notices, phone calls, and other reminders you will have to make to particular persons and groups as the program unfolds. Consider any meetings you plan to hold, such as parent sessions or meetings at which you will be asked to be give reports (e.g., education committee/commission/board meetings), as opportunities to communicate the needed information. Identify them as such in your PR planning and scheduling.

SUMMARY

At first glance the process just outlined may seem complicated. Actually it is mostly common sense. It is hoped that you can already bring to the process certain information and skills: an assessment of any special needs of circumstances in your parish; basic knowledge of developmental theory and what can be expected of a particular age group; a basic awareness of the scope and sequence of the traditional content that needs to be addressed; a grasp of the various methodologies available and their appropriateness for particular age groups; an awareness of the kinds of catechetical resources presently available.

Equipped with this kind of background knowledge you then simply seek to answer the basic programming questions for each group (including parents and catechists for that group): What outcomes do I hope to achieve? What are the best methods and activities for achieving them? What resources and facilities do I need? When can all this be carried out?

Finally, keep in mind that there is nothing wrong with adapting and borrowing from existing programs. Remember, it is not necessary to reinvent the wheel. Just be careful to become totally familiar with any program you adapt or borrow to ensure you fully understand its underlying philosophy and the rationale that explains its content, structure, and processes. The more you are able to make such a program your own, the better you will be able to implement it.

FOR REFLECTION:

1. List all the groups in your parish you are responsible for catechizing. Do you have an adequate goal stated for each?

2. What evaluative procedures will be most functional in your parish setting?

3. Review existing programs in other parishes. What aspects of these programs might you borrow and adapt to meet your own needs?

4 Developmental Stages and Catechetical Structures

The heart of your program for children and youth, of course, is always your curriculum—the information, values, and behaviors you hope to impart. The key to good curriculum development is your understanding of the stages of psychological and faith development. So we want to make a few observations on that topic. Also, because a good curriculum can still be rendered ineffective if it is not packaged within the right structures, we also want to make a few observations about possible catechetical structures.

STAGES OF PSYCHOLOGICAL AND FAITH DEVELOPMENT

In developing a curriculum, the stages of psychological and faith development are too often treated as if they were much the same. In reality, each is quite distinct and presents certain distinct implications for your curriculum.

Psychological stages of development seek to describe the emotional and intellectual capacities at a particular age and are thus closely tied to chronological age. Typically, children and youth in the same age group will also demonstrate very similar capacities. Barring trauma or handicapping conditions, these stages unfold quite predictably. So, for example, if you gather a group of eight year olds, they will be quite similar in their emotional and intellectual development.

This fact makes it possible to identify a group's readiness to deal with certain concepts, and it also suggests the kinds of methods that might be most appropriate. For example, the capacity to gather and memorize information is perhaps at its highest in younger children. Young children possess a unique facility, for instance, to learn new languages, a task that becomes more challenging the older we get. By around age 12, children's capacity to use logic has reached an almost adult level. But at this age their capacity for abstract thinking and spiritual insight is still more or less dormant. Thus they are quite receptive to topics that use logic, such as math and science, but will continue to struggle to grasp a concept like altruism or mercy or to appreciate poetry. By around age 16, however, this capacity for spiritual insight begins to emerge and the youth are ready to begin to deal with reality at a more spiritual or metaphysical level. It is not surprising, therefore, to find that research in psychological development is used extensively in the academic world to construct curriculum programs in languages, literature, math, the physical and social sciences, and so forth.

Research into the theory of faith development, through using the findings of research in psychological development, begins with an understanding of the characteristics of mature faith and then works backward to describe the steps or stages of less mature faith through which one must travel to reach that desired goal.

These stages of less mature faith are tied somewhat precariously to chronological age and psychological development. For example, because fully mature faith depends on fully mature development of emotional and psychological capacities, we cannot expect small children or even junior high youth to achieve it. The best they can do is achieve the level of maturity in faith that their emotional and intellectual capacities can support.

At the same time, it is possible for a person to become fully mature in the psychological sense and yet remain at a stage of faith development more appropriate for a child. Studies show that this is the case for a great many adults.

In terms of your curriculum, then, keep in mind the distinction between these two approaches to development. Stages of faith development will tell you where you want to go and how far you can hope to go in fostering faith in a particular age group. Stages of psychological development will tell you what is appropriate to introduce and how it might best be presented. For example, by age 12 you can hope that most children have moved beyond what the literature has described as mythic-literal faith and have begun to acquire a more affiliative faith. Faith development theory tells you that. Psychological development theory will tell when it is best to begin a more formal study of Scripture or how best to introduce a concept like "sacrament" to eight year olds.

For a good review of how these two stage theories work together and should help shape curriculum development, we suggest you re-read chapter VIII, "Catechesis Toward Maturity in Faith," of *Sharing the Light of Faith: National Catechetical Directory for Catholics of the United States.*

SOME ISSUES OF STRUCTURE: GROUPINGS

One of the tasks involved in program development is to decide how you will group the children and youth. The simplest way, of course, is to mirror the school formula and group them by grade level. In smaller parishes, however, this is not always practical because you could end up with only three or four children in some classes. Some programs maintain grade levels through eighth grade but then group all the high school youth into a single program. But grouping children and youth of different age levels is sometimes like trying to mix oil and water. So if by conviction or necessity you decide to structure your program in other than the grade level format, there are a few guidelines we suggest you keep in mind.

First, as a rule of thumb you will have no problem forming groups made up of children age seven, eight, and nine (grades one-three). Groups made up of ten and eleven year olds (grades four and five) also mix well. Likewise, 12–14 year olds (grades six-eight) can be grouped together, but now you are entering into a more problematic area. The typical 14-year-old girl will be significantly more mature than a typical 12- or 13-year-old boy. In fact, a 14-year-old girl is often significantly more mature than many 14-year-old boys.

This brings us to a second guideline. If you do choose to form groups made up of youth ages 12–14, one method is to form same sex groups by separating boys and girls. A 14-year-old girl can get along quite well with a 12-year-old girl and even be something of a mentor. On the other hand, she will find a 12-year-old boy an annoyance. Also, puberty brings with it all kinds of underlying dynamics that are present when you bring boys and girls of this age together, most of which interfere with any attempts to create an environment of learning, openness, sharing, and community. Simply by separating boys and girls at this age you diffuse much of this electricity and find that the youth become more open and receptive to your catechizing efforts. In fact, studies demonstrate that separating the sexes in catechetical settings is a good idea from seventh through ninth grade. Similar studies now show that students in same sex rather than coed high schools tend to do better academically. However, for purposes of catechetical programming, by about age 15 (tenth grade) boys have tended to catch up with girls in terms of psychological maturity. Putting boys and girls in the same groupings then ceases to be so problematic.

It is becoming more common in parishes to opt for a youth ministry model for high school catechesis, thus grouping all students of high school age together. Some programs now even include junior high youth (seventh and eighth grade) in such a program. Be slow to move into such an arrangement. While it is true that current studies indicate that there should be many similarities in programs for junior high and senior high youth, such as a service component, opportunities for socialization, opportunities to experience liturgy and so forth, there are also important differences to keep in mind. It is mostly a matter of maturity, similar to the situation that dictates separating boys and girls at the junior high level. It is also a sociological issue, rooted in students' perception of themselves in the high school environment. For example, in the high school world, seniors and juniors rarely socialize with ninth and tenth graders. In fact, most tenth graders do not socialize with ninth graders.

So if you do choose to form any "total high school" groupings, you will want to give certain roles, privileges, and responsibilities to the older students that the younger students still must "earn." As much as possible, structure your program so that the older students assume the role of mentor to the younger students, much like how the old one-room schoolhouse functions. Older students can serve as facilitators in small group discussions. They can serve as "project directors" if you program service activities into your curriculum. Selected older students can be asked to give "witness talks" to younger students on topics like gangs, drugs, sexuality, and the like. Older students can assume the role of aide to catechists in certain activities. Also, periodically, you should hold sessions just for the older students to deal with issues or concerns not yet experienced by the younger youth.

In short, in forming your groupings keep in mind the significant differences in psychological development that can be present in children or youth only one or two years apart in age. If you remember to take these differences into account when you form your groupings, you can avoid a great deal of frustration later on.

OTHER POSSIBLE STRUCTURES

There is much in the literature about using an intergenerational structure in which you bring groups of children, youth, and adults together. In the same way, you hear much about a family-centered model. Finally, there is a strong movement toward Lectionary-based catechesis, which uses the yearly cycle of liturgical readings as the foundation for a curriculum.

Each is a valid approach and under the proper circumstances can be more effective than some of our more traditional models. However, none is a panacea, primarily because the success of each requires certain conditions in order to be effective. For example, you will need to gain the cooperation of a large number of adults, especially parents, for the intergenerational model to work. Also, this approach requires a larger number of well-trained facilitators to function effectively. Finding and training such facilitators can be every bit as challenging as finding and training catechists.

In the same way, a family-centered approach can be very effective with some parents, but experience shows that many parents will choose not to participate. Therefore, parishes that employ a family-centered structure usually find it necessary to also maintain a more traditional program to ensure that most children and youth will be ministered to.

The Lectionary-based model is more controversial. It is challenged, for example, on the premise that the Lectionary is too inconsistent to provide a truly comprehensive curriculum. Certain topics central to the faith receive too little attention, according to the critics. Critics also argue that the methodology employed in this approach (discussion and reflection) is not always suitable for younger children. Finally they argue that the approach presupposes regular, year-long attendance at the Sunday liturgy to be effective. In most parishes attendance by many parents and children does not reflect that ideal.

Though supporters can argue effectively against these objections, this approach requires some special attention. For example, to be able to facilitate this approach effectively, most catechists would need to be retrained. It will be necessary to supplement the Lectionary-based material with other resources, so the task of curriculum development is not totally avoided. Essential programs like sacramental preparation do not fit easily into this structure and usually have to be programmed in a more traditional way. Regular, year-long attendance at liturgy by parents and children is a problem that would need to be addressed.

As stated, it is possible to meet all these requirements, and some parishes have successfully developed a program of catechesis around the Lectionary-based format. Typically, these parishes tend to have a strong sense of community and strong pastoral leadership present. Keep that in mind if you are considering this format in your programming.

As a rule of thumb, if you are considering one of these formats, we suggest you maintain a more traditional structure and initiate the format as a pilot, inviting interested parents to participate. This will enable you to better assess what is needed to make it effective and if it is, in fact, a feasible approach for the entire parish.

SUMMARY

Especially in the task of developing a curriculum, a knowledge and understanding of the stages of psychological and faith development is essential. It is equally important that you recognize the distinct roles each plays in formulating your curriculum. How you group students also is a key consideration in programming. We have suggested some guidelines to help you avoid certain common mistakes in this regard. Finally, in considering less traditional formats, such as intergenerational or Lectionary-based catechesis, move cautiously. Any of these can be effective, provided you address the special needs and problems each presents. So study the pros and cons carefully before you act, and consider beginning with a pilot project rather than adopting a full-blown program.

FOR REFLECTION:

1. Evaluate the present way you have formed age groupings of children and youth in light of the principles described above. If you identify any problem areas, what adjustments might you make?

2. In your program, is it possible to separate boys and girls at the seventh, eighth, and/or ninth grade levels? Do you think it is desirable?

3. If you are considering using one of the alternative formats (e.g., Lectionary-based catechesis), list all the possible pros and cons involved. Also, identify and then arrange to visit other parishes already employing that format.

5 Programming for Adults

While many of the principles of program development we have been describing can be applied
equally to programming for all age groups—
children, youth, and adults—there are some special
considerations when developing a catechetical program
for adults. We will explore them in this chapter.

For starters, it is relatively easy to form groupings of
children and youth. We have the traditional chronological
age or class year formula that for the most part ensures a
particular group will share the same needs and capacities.
This makes it rather easy to establish goals and desired
outcomes that can be applied to the total group. Adults
cannot be grouped that easily. Granted, most adults in a
particular age range may share certain similar interests and
needs, but this is by no means guaranteed. This makes it
quite difficult to establish any workable statement of goals
and outcomes.

Also, attendance can be made more or less mandatory
for children and youth. Attendance by adults is much
more fluid. In fact the single most common complaint
regarding adult catechesis is how often even the best
planned, promoted, and implemented adult education event
has poor attendance. The pressures of time that most
adults experience today is certainly one reason for this, but
there are other factors to consider as we will see shortly.

Finally, despite all the documents, literature, and official
statements that proclaim that catechesis is a lifelong

process, this message has yet to be adequately heard and understood. We still labor under the long-standing idea that catechesis is about teaching truths rather than about growth in discipleship. So as long as adults feel they "know enough about the faith" they will not feel the need for attending formal catechetical programs.

A PROPOSED STARTING POINT

As with programming for any group, the starting point needs to be a clear mission statement or at least a statement of the overall goal for adult catechesis. The following is a sample of such a mission or goal statement:

> The adult catechesis program at St. Matthew parish seeks to promote ongoing opportunities for continuing conversion and growth toward mature discipleship and to provide for those opportunities.

Such a statement goes a long way toward guiding the development of an effective catechetical program for adults. It clearly focuses on mature discipleship as the goal. This is a much richer and comprehensive goal than merely seeking to develop informed adults.

Because discipleship development involves such a wide variety of elements and because there is a certain unique quality to each adult's faith journey, both the focus and the format for growth in adult disciples (that is, adult catechesis broadly understood) needs to be understood as embracing a wide scope of activities and experiences. Growth can take place both by involvement in ministry and by being ministered to. It can involve both serving and being served, teaching and being taught, and praying and being prayed for. Thus, opportunities for adult catechesis can range from taking a formal course of study in theology to helping out at the local food pantry. At one stage in the adult's faith journey it may mean participating in a marriage preparation program as an engaged couple. At another stage it may involve helping to lead a marriage preparation program. And at still another stage it may involve receiving marriage counseling.

Note, therefore, that the task in the above mission statement is identified as both to promote and to provide. The implication here is that many opportunities for conversion and growth in discipleship already exist in the parish. Even a partial list of the typical activities of a parish reveals this:

- Participation in the parish's sacramental life: as worshiper, a liturgical minister, as catechist in a sacramental preparation program, as a parent whose child is involved in sacramental preparation, as a participant or catechist in the RCIA program, etc.

- Participation in ministry and ministry training: liturgical ministry, catechetical ministry, social concerns ministry, evangelization ministry, leadership (councils, committees, boards), Vincent de Paul Society, Stephen and Elizabeth ministry, bereavement ministry, etc.

- Participation in specific programs, services, groups, and devotions: family life program, small Christian community groups, informal prayer and Scripture study groups, various support groups (bereavement, single parent, addiction), parish retreats and missions, marriage encounter programs, etc.

A good adult program, therefore, will first focus much of its energy simply on helping promote participation in these kinds of activities, rather than in "running" them. If the goal is in fact an overall growth in discipleship, opportunities for such growth already abound in most parishes and do not have to be reinvented. By cooperating with and supporting such adult activities rather than adding to the list, you avoid the trap of competing for the time and attention of adults in your own programming.

The mission statement requires that you also provide opportunities. The ones you provide should seek to fill the gaps and to address needs and interests not already being met by existing parish programs. A parish retreat is usually a wonderful growth opportunity. If no other group is responsible for planning such an event, that can become something your adult program seeks to provide. Based on your needs assessment you may discover certain ad hoc adult concerns not being addressed by any other group in the parish, such as coping with adolescent children or the emergence of youth gangs in the area. Offering adults an opportunity to view such an issue in the light of the Gospel would be an appropriate part of your adult program at this time.

Since formal study in areas like theology, Scripture, spirituality, or a current Church document will always be an important aspect of growth in discipleship for various adults at certain points in their faith journey, these remain a traditional part in adult programming. However, remember that such highly focused topics will seldom attract large numbers. There is no need to be discouraged by this once you realize that many adults are already participating in the many other parish activities that foster growth in discipleship. Formal study is just one of these.

In summary, many of the problems usually associated with program development for adults can be eliminated if you have a clear understanding of the purpose of adult catechesis and can form a clear mission or goal statement that expresses what you hope to achieve.

SOME BASIC PRINCIPLES TO CONSIDER

In addition to the role of your mission statement as a guiding force, there are some underlying principles related to adulthood in general and adult catechesis in particular that affect your ability to foster growth toward mature discipleship. These can be summarized as follows:

- Adults experience several distinct psychological stages as they move through the adult life cycle from their early adulthood to their senior years. Each stage impacts on the way one grows in discipleship. The implication here is that you seek to deepen your familiarity of the stages of adult development and remain sensitive to them when you plan specific programs and events. For example, a couple just beginning a family will have different needs and interests than a couple who have raised their children and are experiencing the "empty nest" syndrome.

- Faith, and therefore discipleship, also goes through distinct stages of development. Once again it is important to be familiar with these stages of faith development, together with the characteristics and needs of those in each par-ticular stage. Chronological age is not the criti-cal factor here. Adults in their fifties can still be at a stage of faith more appropriate for young children, and a 30 year old can possibly possess a very advanced level of faith development.

- Adults must assume responsibility for their own growth in discipleship. They cannot be coerced, and they should not be manipulated. We must also accept the fact that some adults will simply choose not to strive for growth in

discipleship no matter how sincerely you invite
and seek to motivate them.

• Adult learning is governed by certain principles
(referred to as andragogy) that are quite distinct
from the principles that govern how a child
learns (referred to as pedagogy). Though you
may already be familiar with these principles
we will review them briefly below.

• The role and context of the faith community is
a critical factor in fostering mature discipleship.
The community is needed to provide the adult
with a visible witness of lived discipleship. It
also provides the ongoing invitation, appropriate challenges, and concrete opportunities for
growth. It is safe to say that the more vital the
overall faith life of the local parish, the more
effective will be your own efforts in achieving
the goals of adult catechesis.

• The small group setting is an especially effective format for fostering mature faith. In fact,
in planning and structuring events for adults,
try to use the small group format whenever
possible. Though some adults will prefer a more
formal, anonymous setting, the majority of
adults today are open to, and in fact hunger for,
the intimacy, sense of belonging, opportunity
to share, and the more informal, spontaneous
atmosphere found in the small group setting.

• Personal invitation and mentoring play a criti-
cal role in motivating adults and maintaining
their participation in activities that foster
growth in discipleship. The validity of this
principle can be traced all the way back to the
Gospel and the life of the early Church.

As you reflect on these principles you will begin to see many practical implications for your program development. These principles suggest many good programming questions, such as: How can I better include the element of personal invitation into my programming? Into what present activities can I introduce the small group format? What is the present faith development level of the group for which I am planning? What is a realistic attendance for this activity? By using these principles and the questions they suggest you will be able to avoid many common mistakes in programming for adults and also help them to build many effective qualities.

A REVIEW OF THE PRINCIPLES
OF ANDRAGOGY

There are several important distinctions between the child as learner and the adult as learner. For example, children are expected to learn; it is their most important duty. Adults choose to learn. What the child should learn is determined almost entirely by others. What the adult learns is determined by the adult's choices. Children learn to prepare for future tasks. Adults learn because they seek to meet some immediate need or interest. Given these kinds of distinctions, here is a review of several important principles of andragogy that govern how adults learn.

• Adults decide for themselves what they want to learn, when to learn, and how to go about learning it. This is the single most important principle related to adult attendance at events you might establish. If adults do not like a topic, when it is offered, or how you propose to present it, they simply will not attend. This principle also suggests the importance of

polling adult interests periodically before
establishing programs.

- Adults typically set their own goals. They seek
  out information and skills that for the most
  part have immediate use or that can help them
  meet some immediate need they are experiencing. Like the above principle, this one points
  to the importance of attempting to discern the
  needs and interests of the adults in your parish.

- Adults bring a great deal of experience to the
  learning situation and expect to be able to use
  and to share that experience. They likewise
  expect their experience to be respected and
  valued. Conversely, they resent it when the
  presenter or instructor displays an autocratic,
  condescending attitude. If given the opportunity,
  adults therefore prefer to participate in the
  learning process and to share information
  rather than to sit passively and be told what they
  need to know. They expect the opportunity to
  challenge, add to, and comment on what is
  being shared. Be sure to take these points into
  account when structuring an adult learning
  experience, whether it is a catechist training
  session, a parent meeting, or a formal course.

- Adults do their own evaluating of the success
  or failure of a learning experience. If it met
  their needs and was conducted in an engaging
  way, it was successful, even if the event did not
  meet some of the specific goals you had established. Therefore, always seek immediate feedback from adult participants after an event.
  Their comments and insights will be invaluable
  in planning future events.

- Adults expect to be treated as adults. Therefore, do not patronize them or burden them
with too many rules. Allow them to take the
initiative and to offer suggestions when
problems occur.

- Adults expect some degree of comfort and
convenience in the learning situation. Their
attendance usually has already come at the
expense of some degree of sacrifice. A conve-
nient location and time, an appropriate room
temperature, a good sound system, adequate
lighting, comfortable seating, easily acquired
resources and materials—all these are important considerations in your planning. A child
will continue to attend, despite inconvenience
and discomfort, because he or she has no
choice. After encountering inconvenience and
discomfort the first time, an adult will simply
choose to stay home the next time.

- Finally, adults tend to resist change simply for
the sake of change. They need to be convinced
that a new approach or theory is better than
the one they have already spent considerable
time acquiring and using successfully. Therefore, if you are seeking to effect some significant change in thinking and behavior in adults
(a conversion?) you need to plan more carefully,
building into the process ample time for participants to discuss, explore, challenge, and test
out these new ideas. Also, you need to show
appropriate respect for the deeply held convictions you are asking the adults to let go of.

While the above principles may already be familiar
to you, refer to them often when engaged in program

development for adults. To ignore them is to doom even the most well-intentioned program to failure. Following these principles seldom means changing your goals. It just means changing how you propose to accomplish them.

A WORD ABOUT PERSONAL INVITATION AND MENTORING

In the area of adult catechesis, much has been written about the importance of promotion or "advertising" your programs and events effectively. While attractive brochures, timely parish bulletin announcements, and the like have definite roles, studies indicate that the most effective promotion for adults is personal invitation. On the one hand, people find it affirming to be asked by a friend to participate. On the other hand, people find it is more difficult to ignore a personal invitation than it is to ignore an impersonal brochure or bulletin announcement.

In the same way, one of the more effective ways to minister to adults is through mentoring. It goes beyond offering a personal invitation to offering personal, ongoing guidance and support. This principle is being applied effectively in many programs intended for adults, like marriage and baptismal preparation. It is the driving force behind the success of programs like Elizabeth Ministry, Stephen Ministry, and Befrienders. It has been used effectively by Alcoholics Anonymous. Therefore, as you develop programs, consider ways you might utilize personal invitations and mentoring.

SUMMARY

Properly understood program development for adults is not as difficult as it might seem. As with all program development, the key is to formulate a clear statement of your mission or goal. As much as possible, include existing parish activities for adults in your programming. Do periodic needs assessment. Respect the principles cited at the beginning of the chapter and the principles of andragogy. Be sensitive to the various stages of faith. By following these suggestions you can avoid many of the pitfalls related to programming for adults.

FOR REFLECTION:

1. Review the mission or goal statement for your parish's adult catechesis. Is it adequate, or does it need revision? List all the programs and activities in your parish that can be considered opportunities for adults to grow in discipleship. How can you best incorporate these into your programming for adults?

2. How can you better incorporate the small group structure into your adult programming? How might you better use mentoring?

Conclusion

As you can see, the task of program development really does call on all your skills and background as a DRE. Having established a clear goal or mission statement, you proceed to answer the programming questions: What is needed by a particular age group and when? What is the best way to meet those needs? What resources and facilities are called for? We've attempted to describe the actual elements and components involved in answering those questions in chapter two, and in chapter three we looked at the step-by-step process involved in putting it all together. Finally, in the last two chapters we suggested some special considerations to keep in mind in programming for children, youth, and adults.

Having reviewed all this material it should be clear that, as complicated as it may seem at first, much of what is involved is basically common sense. Also, throughout this booklet we continually stress one important principle: You do not have to reinvent the wheel. Many excellent programs already exist from which you can borrow and adapt as needed. So, equipped with the suggestions in this booklet, your own common sense, and by borrowing from those who have gone before you, catechetical programming is something you should be able to approach with confidence.

For Further Reading

Catechism of the Catholic Church. Chicago: Loyola Press, 1994.

Connell, Martin, ed. *The Catechetical Documents.* Chicago: Liturgy Training Publications, 1996.

Darcy-Berube, Francoise. *Religious Education at the Crossroads.* Mahwah, NJ: Paulist Press, 1995.

DeVillers, Sylvia, and Jim DeBoy. *How to Choose Catechetical Textbooks.* Washington, DC: NCCL, 1996.

Diocese of Green Bay. *The Green Bay Plan.* 1971.

Elias, John L. *Psychology and Religious Education,* 3rd ed. Melbourne, FL: Krieger Publishing Co., 1990.

Groome, Thomas. *Christian Religious Education: Sharing Our Story and Vision.* San Francisco: Harper San Francisco, 1982.

International Council for Catechesis. *Adult Catechesis in the Christian Community.* Vatican City: Libreria Editrice Vaticana, 1990.

Mauren, Mary La Course. *Creating Communities of Good News: A Handbook for Small Group Facilitators.* Kansas City: Sheed and Ward, 1992.

National Conference of Catholic Bishops. *Sharing the Light of Faith: National Catechetical Directory for Catholics of the United States.* Washington, D.C.: United States Catholic Conference, 1979 (especially chapters V and VIII).

Tighe, Jeanne, and Karen Szentkeresti. *Rethinking Adult Religious Education.* Mahwah, NJ: Paulist Press, 1989.

NOTES